Polly Bee
makes honey

KANEPRESS
AN IMPRINT OF ASTRA BOOKS FOR YOUNG READERS
New York

For Harry, Ed, and Immy—*DC*

For Lynda, Ariadne, and Lola—*JG*

Text copyright © 2021 by Deborah Chancellor
Illustrations copyright © 2021 by Julia Groves
Bee consultant: Rowan Green

First published in the United States in 2024 by Kane Press,
an imprint of Astra Books for Young Readers, a division of Astra Publishing House
astrapublishinghouse.com
Printed in China

Originally published in Great Britain in 2021
by Scallywag Press, London

Library of Congress Cataloging-in-Publication Data
Names: Chancellor, Deborah, author. | Groves, Julia, illustrator.
Title: Polly Bee makes honey / by Deborah Chancellor ; illustrated by Julia Groves
Description: First American edition. | New York : Kane Press, an Imprint of Astra
Books For Young Readers, 2024 | Series: Follow my food | Audience:
Ages 2-5 | Audience: Grades K-1 | Summary: "A child narrator tells the story of Polly, a honeybee; she works for her hive and queen and collects pollen and nectar to make honey. Back matter includes a matching game, different species of bees, a kid-friendly recipe, and additional information"-- Provided by publisher.
Identifiers: LCCN 2023020204 (print) | LCCN 2023020205 (ebook) | ISBN 9781662670664 (hardcover) | ISBN 9781662670657 (epub)
Subjects: LCSH: Honeybee--Juvenile literature. | Honey--Juvenile literature. | Bee culture--Juvenile literature.
Classification: LCC SF523.5 .C43 2022 (print) | LCC SF523.5 (ebook) | DDC 595.79/9--dc23/eng/20230516
LC record available at https://lccn.loc.gov/2023020204
LC ebook record available at https://lccn.loc.gov/2023020205

First American edition, 2024

10 9 8 7 6 5 4 3 2 1

Design by Ness Wood.
The text is set in Foundry Sans Medium.
The title is hand lettered.
The illustrations are created in cut paper and digital media.

Polly Bee
makes honey

by Deborah Chancellor
illustrated by Julia Groves

KANE PRESS

New York

Polly is a worker bee.
She makes me delicious honey.

Polly and her sisters work hard for their queen bee.

They collect pollen and nectar from flowers.

Polly's brothers are drone bees.
They're all devoted to their queen.

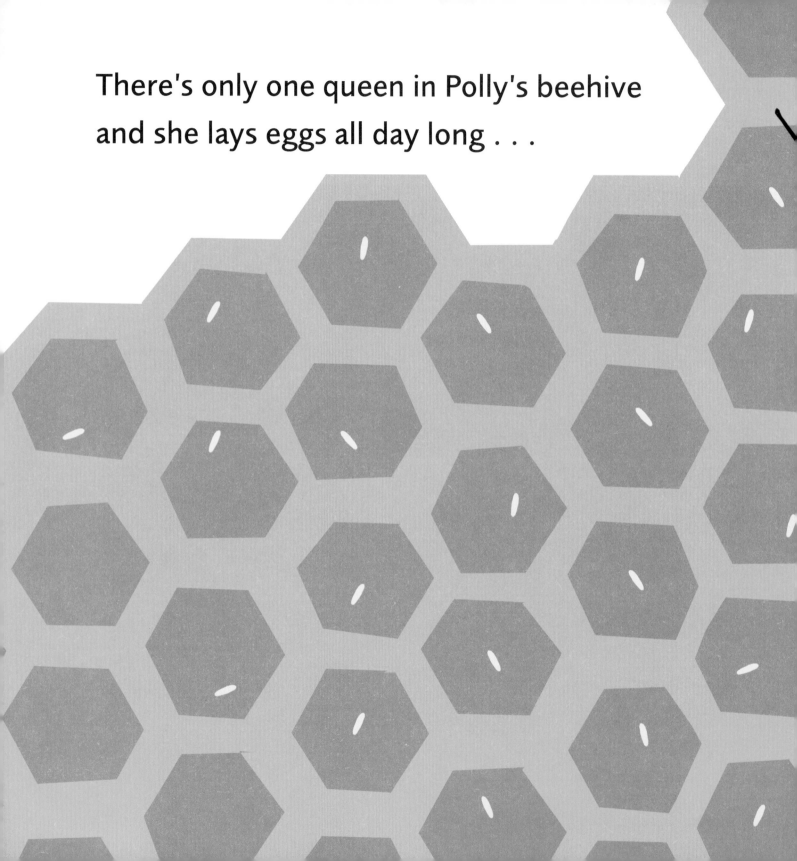

There's only one queen in Polly's beehive
and she lays eggs all day long . . .

Every day, Polly flies
to a faraway meadow.
She sucks sweet nectar
from colorful flowers.

Polly also picks up pollen from the flowers. She brushes it into baggy baskets on her back legs.

Polly zips back home with her heavy load.

Her fine pollen helps feed
the baby bees inside the hive.

Polly squirts the nectar into
the beautiful golden honeycomb.
It thickens into gloopy, gooey honey.

A beekeeper takes care of Polly's beehive.
I help him collect her precious honey.

Making honey is hard work.
I won't waste
a single spoonful!

Follow Polly's pollen trail to match the words and pictures.

A honeycomb is a wall of wax cells where bees store their honey. In winter, bees eat their honey to survive until spring.

A drone bee is a male who mates with the queen bee.

Nectar is the sweet liquid in flowers.

Pollen is the colorful powder in flowers.

A queen bee lays eggs. She's the oldest and biggest bee in the hive.

A worker bee is a female who finds food and protects the hive.

Guess what?

Worker bees tell each other where to find the best flowers by doing a waggle dance outside their beehive. They move around in a figure eight, showing their sisters which direction they must take and how far they need to fly.

We need bees

When bees carry pollen between flowering plants, helping them make seeds, which grow into new plants. Without the help of bees, we would soon run out of food to eat. Many bees are in danger from pollution, pesticides, and the loss of wildflower meadows.

All bees gather nectar and pollen. Most live alone, but honeybees live together, making honey in their hives. You can help them by planting bee-friendly flowers and herbs, such as clover and thyme. Different bees like different flower shapes— each bee always flies to her favorite!

Different bees

There are around 20,000 species of bees. This is more than all the species of mammals and birds in the world. But only around 40 species of bee actually make honey. Honeybees live in every continent except Antarctica.

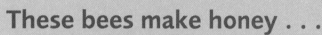

These bees make honey . . .

red dwarf honeybee

western honeybee

giant honeybee

These bees don't . . .

carpenter bee

nomad bee

blue orchard bee

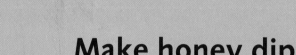
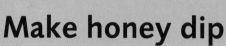

Make honey dip

We can use honey to sweeten our food.
Ask a grown-up to help you make this
creamy honey dip. It tastes great
with slices of crisp apple.

You will need:

6 tablespoons sour cream
6 tablespoons plain Greek yogurt
1 tablespoon honey
1/4 teaspoon cinnamon
2 sliced apples

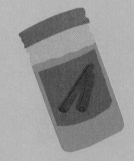

Instructions:

 1. Pour sour cream and yogurt in a bowl.

2. Stir the mixture.

3. Add honey and cinnamon and mix well.

4. Dip in your apple slices.

5. Enjoy your sweet snack!

Do your part

We really need bees, but their habitats are disappearing. Make a wildlife garden at home or school to give them food and shelter. Choose plants they love and don't use any poison sprays.

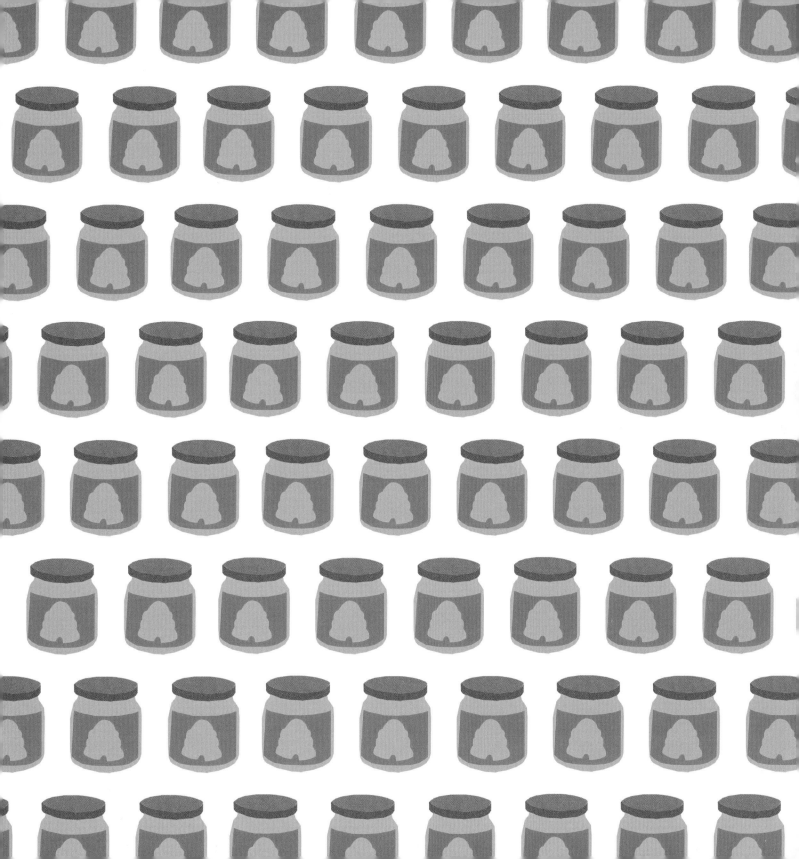

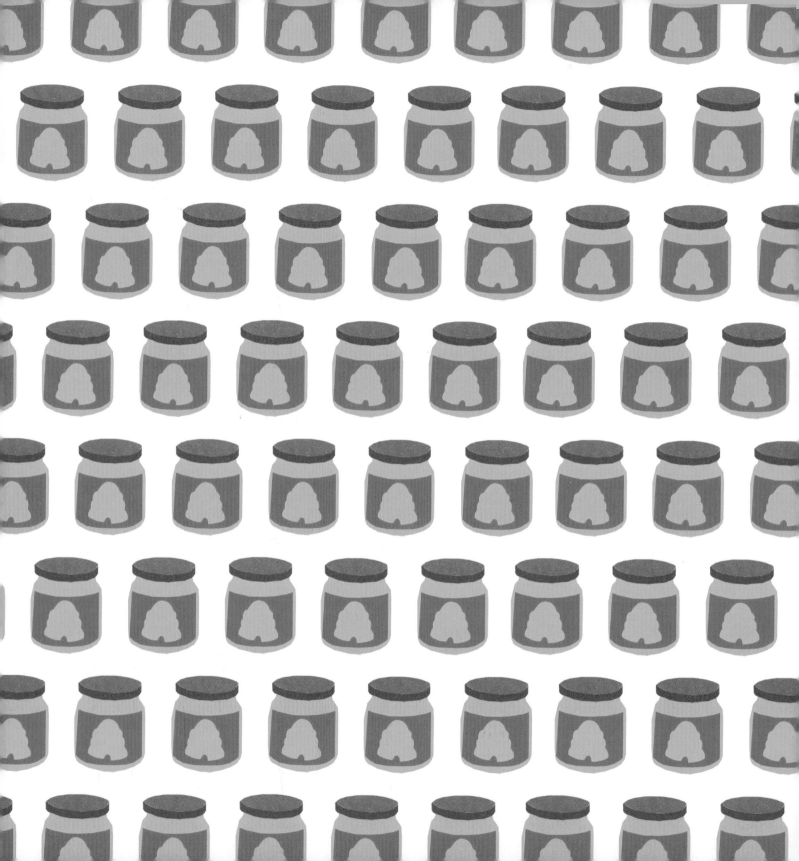